My House is a Lighthouse

Stories of Lighthouses and Their Keepers

Christine Welldon

NIMBUS
PUBLISHING
— NIMBUS.CA —

Nimbus Publishing Limited
3660 Strawberry Hill, Halifax, NS, B3K 5A9
(902) 455-4286 nimbus.ca

Printed and bound in Canada

NB1441

Cover design: Heather Bryan
Interior design: Andrew Herygers
Editor: Emily MacKinnon

Library and Archives Canada Cataloguing in Publication
Title: My house is a lighthouse : stories of lighthouses and their keepers
Welldon, Christine, author.
Compass series | Includes bibliographical references and index.
Canadiana 20189068779
ISBN 9781771087568 (softcover)
LCSH: Lighthouse keepers—Juvenile literature. | LCSH: Lighthouses—Juvenile literature.
LCC VK1010 .W45 2019   DDC j387.1   55—dc23

Nimbus Publishing acknowledges the financial support for its publishing activities from the Government of Canada, the Canada Council for the Arts, and from the Province of Nova Scotia. We are pleased to work in partnership with the Province of Nova Scotia to develop and promote our creative industries for the benefit of all Nova Scotians.

Dedicated to the lightkeepers—ever brave, resilient, and steadfast.

Light the lantern, keep it burning,
Many ships are sailing home…

—"The Lighthouse Keeper"
by James Puntis, 1878

Table of Contents

Note: Look up terms in **bold** in the glossary on page 103.

Introduction

WANTED! LIGHTKEEPER

IF YOU ARE DEPENDABLE AND WILLING TO LIVE IN AN ISOLATED PLACE; WORK SHIFTS AROUND THE CLOCK IN STORMS, SLEET, ICE, AND POUNDING WAVES; IF YOU KNOW FIRST AID AND ARE ABLE TO TRAVEL BY BOAT OR HELICOPTER, WE WANT YOU!

Can you imagine yourself as a lightkeeper? Could you live full-time on the rough margin where the land meets the sea? You might find yourself working from a rocky clifftop or sandy shoal, perched on a stony beach or tucked into a sheltered bay. Wherever you are, your important job is to keep the light shining as it flashes its warm message of welcome and safe harbour: *Find help and comfort from the storm. Here, you have a friend.* The light also sends warnings of jagged rocks and treacherous **reefs** nearby: *STAY AWAY! BEWARE! DANGER! THIS IS NOT A DRILL!*

Lighthouse or Light Station?

"Lighthouse" refers to a tower with a light beam at the top.

"Light station" includes a lighthouse, but also dwellings, a foghorn building, helipad, solar panels, and other equipment needed to run the station.

Hundreds of light stations no longer have full-time keepers to welcome and protect mariners. Sadly, lighthouses are being automated, and their keepers have become just like an endangered species. There once were eight hundred and seventy-five staffed light stations across North America. Men and women keepers lived at these stations year-round to clock the wind speeds, report weather conditions, and ensure the safety of the big ships and small crafts at sea.

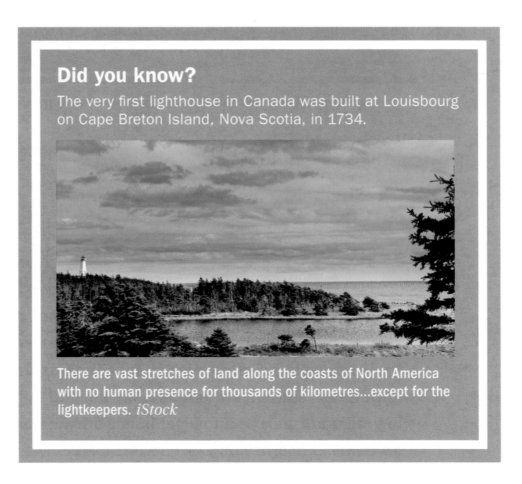

Did you know?

The very first lighthouse in Canada was built at Louisbourg on Cape Breton Island, Nova Scotia, in 1734.

There are vast stretches of land along the coasts of North America with no human presence for thousands of kilometres...except for the lightkeepers. *iStock*

My House is a Lighthouse

Today, there are just fifty-one staffed lighthouses remaining in Canada, and only one in the United States. **Skeletal towers** with computerized lights have sprung up where once proud lighthouse keepers and their families kept watch, lived, and played. These automatic lights flash warnings, but they are simply machines. They cannot reach out, as their keepers once did, to rescue fishers and small boats from danger.

Some of the working lightkeepers you will meet in these pages yearn for the sound of the helicopter coming to take them home at the end of a long and lonely shift. Others can think of no better place to be than their remote and rugged station. All feel a devotion to being of service and having a fine purpose in life.

Valued by their communities, they have stayed on to fulfill their time-old mission:

Keep the light shining.

Be ever watchful.

Help those in trouble on the sea.

CHAPTER 1
A Haunting Beauty

Cape Beale, British Columbia

Light characteristic: flashing white every 5 seconds.
Foghorn signal: every 60 seconds.

Cape Beale lies alone at the end of the West Coast Trail, a challenging hiking path. *marinas.com*

A calm and sparkling ocean is the sailor's delight. But at Cape Beale, an impish wave can upset a beautiful day, and a sailor's boat, in minutes.

Perched high above the Pacific Ocean on the west coast of Vancouver Island, this **Heritage Lighthouse** has stunning views of blue crashing waves and emerald green forests. But its waters

My House is a Lighthouse

have been nicknamed "The Graveyard of the Pacific" for good reason. The shore is fringed with dangerous reefs and monster waves can swallow entire canoes in a second. These waves are called *chup-meek*, a word of the Huu-ay-aht people, who live on and around Cape Beale, that means "canoe swallowers."

Splash. Gulp. And it's over.

Cape Beale's lightkeeper, Karen, keeps a sharp watch for mariners who have surprise run-ins with chup-meek waves. Karen works twelve-hour shifts, each one beginning at 3:30 A.M.

Down by the shore one day, Karen's assistant keeper heard someone yelling for help through the fog. A small boat bobbed upside-down on the water,

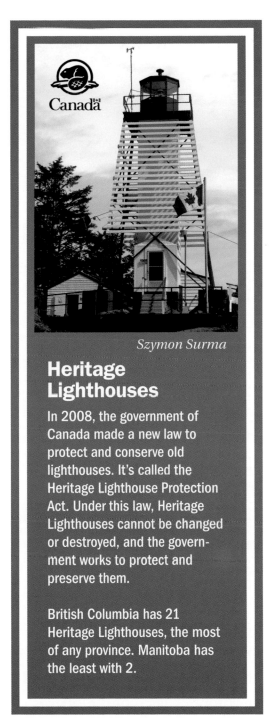

Szymon Surma

Heritage Lighthouses

In 2008, the government of Canada made a new law to protect and conserve old lighthouses. It's called the Heritage Lighthouse Protection Act. Under this law, Heritage Lighthouses cannot be changed or destroyed, and the government works to protect and preserve them.

British Columbia has 21 Heritage Lighthouses, the most of any province. Manitoba has the least with 2.

A Haunting Beauty

Keeper Karen finds a quiet moment to relax with her dog, Pepper. *Karen*

flipped by a rogue wave. Like a cat tossing a mouse, the chup-meek had tipped its three passengers into the ocean. One man struggled to free himself from the bow, his face was cut, and he had broken two ribs.

"The weather happened too suddenly for them to put out a **mayday** call," explains Karen. "If [my] assistant hadn't heard their screams, they would not have survived."

Karen is used to these sudden emergencies. "Keeping watch and listening to the radio for distress calls is a big part of our job," she says. "But mariners sometimes don't have radio communication, or the signal is just not strong enough. We get heavy seas when pictures on the wall rattle, the windows

Wild weather can toss small boats onto rocks within seconds. *Megan Thomas*

shake and chatter like crazy. Lightning can strike the tower, knock out electrical systems, and cause damage."

Sometimes Karen has to deal with special weather like waterspouts. These powerful storms are tornadoes that form over the water, creating twirling **funnels** that can tip and sink small boats in seconds.

"In one storm, down in the weather room the **anemometer** spun from 40 to 73 knots in mere minutes when some waterspouts hit us," she says. "Two waterspouts went by, a dangerous situation for small boats. We've seen sailboats get knocked down by the force of these funnels."

A Haunting Beauty

Wish Granted!

Karen is used to the ocean and its ever-changing weather. She and her husband, Kyle, once lived on a sailboat but after eight years afloat, they were both ready to live on solid ground at last.

"I wanted to own a compost heap and a clothesline," Karen laughs. To have both those things by the sea would be even better.

A marine career was the natural next step. The couple took a course with the **Canadian Coast Guard** and was all set for new adventures. While Kyle worked in Search and Rescue, Karen looked for lightkeeper work. Her dream of living on land soon came true when she took the job at Cape Beale. And it even came with a compost heap and a clothesline!

Karen and Kyle love practical jokes. Steve Beale is happy to help. *Karen*

My House is a Lighthouse

Steve Beale

"Steve" is a training dummy that washed ashore one day from a Search and Rescue boat. Karen and Kyle love practical jokes. They put Steve to good use to surprise the many visitors to Cape Beale.

"We leave him out sometimes to scare visitors," laughs Karen. "One time we dressed him up in a wig, glasses, a pair of socks, a robe, and put him on the toilet in the guest cottage. A guest went to use the toilet and when he didn't return I went out to look for him, worried he'd had a heart attack at sight of Steve."

She found him pacing outside the cottage. "Some strange lady is in there," the guest said. "I'm waiting for her to come out."

You can imagine their laughter when the truth was told!

The Blue Hiker

Cape Beale lies at the end of the 22-kilometre West Coast Trail, a pathway full of muddy stretches, log crossings, exposed tree roots, and tidal flats. Hikers sometimes turn up at the Cape Beale Lighthouse with broken bones or sprains from a long day's walk. But there is one hiker who is shrouded in mystery to this day.

"There was a keeper here for thirty-three years," says Karen, "who talked about the 'Blue Hiker'—a young man wearing blue jeans, carrying a blue backpack. The keeper saw the hiker several times. He walked along the boardwalk, past the kitchen window, but then just disappeared. The keeper would look for him out of the living room window. But somehow, no one was there."

11

But such stories are not uncommon.

"My friend Patti was doing relief work here and heard a vacuum cleaner turn itself on in the basement," says Karen. "Another friend woke up to hear the toilet flushing by itself. No one else was home."

Ghostly people wearing old-fashioned clothing have also been seen dancing in the keeper's living room.

Cape Beale has a long history. Built in 1874, it is the oldest staffed light station on the west coast of Canada. Perhaps its former keepers just like to come back for a visit now and again!

What's for Dinner?

Karen loves the quiet moments on Cape Beale. "Being immersed in nature out here is a big part of what I love about my job. Blue jays greet me in the morning and I have a big garden."

The "flying supermarket" delivers Karen's monthly food order. *Chris Roberts*

Once every month, a helicopter with their food supplies delivers their groceries, just like a flying supermarket.

"We radio in our orders and receive our monthly groceries by helicopter." If they run out of food before the month's end, there is always a harvest from the land and sea. "When the tide's out, our dinner table is set as if by magic," says Karen. "We harvest mussels, go crabbing, fish salmon, pick cranberries in the bog, and hunt for mushrooms."

When It's Quiet...

Life on Cape Beale has its quiet moments when the weather is calm and the sea is peaceful. During such times, Karen likes to watch the dolphins and whales at play. "I really have a love for these creatures," she says. And beachcombing turns up some exciting finds.

"My husband builds furniture with found lumber on the beach. One time, a big fir log washed up. I sat on that

Kash the lighthouse cat takes in the view.
Karen

Visitors to Cape Beale enjoy sweeping ocean views. *Dale Simonson*

log, kissed that log, and said, 'You're gonna be in in my house one day!'

"Now it's been turned into a beautiful island for my kitchen!"

Karen's family members come to this island getaway every summer to soak up the view and salty air.

"A young friend of mine writes sea poems about lighthouses. She uses pencil and paper. I won't give the kids the Wi-Fi password. I tell them, 'No smartphones allowed on Cape Beale!'"

And who needs a smartphone when nature's voice is always calling?

My House is a Lighthouse

CHAPTER 2
It's Not Easy Being Green

Green Island, British Columbia

Light characteristic: flashing white every 5 seconds.
Foghorn signal: foghorn no longer in use.

Green Island is a place of barren rock, scrubby weeds, and angry winds.
Chris Roberts

Not much is green on Green Island. Visitors will see a carefully tended lawn and some scrubby weeds clinging to barren soil, but the rest is grey rock swept clean by angry winds. Green Island's light station is high above the treeline and the furthest north of all stations in Canada, close to the Alaska border.

"On our island there are no trees," says Keeper Barney, "but we do share the island with about three thousand seagulls every summer, and in spring and fall, we get visited by ten bald eagles."

15

While it seems like a bleak place, Green Island's colourful red-and-white station welcomes sailors entering Canadian waters from the north. Now a Heritage Lighthouse, it offers a cheerful sight to mariners heading up the **Inside Passage** to Alaska or across the Pacific Ocean to Asia.

Green Island's lighthouse. *Chris Roberts*

Shiver Me Timbers

In winter, winds howl down from Alaska, and icy seas pound the light station. Gales sweeping the island can spring up in a second. Back in the early days, the story goes that one lightkeeper's wife had to pin her children to the clothesline to keep them from being blown out to sea. Another keeper, out on the water in his boat, was blown north for over one hundred **nautical miles** after his engine failed. He landed not far from Ketchican, Alaska!

My House is a Lighthouse

Ice and snow covers the only patch of lawn on Green Island. *Barney*

Keeper Barney's station has been rocked by hurricane-force winds that gust up to 145 kilometres per hour. Freezing rains sculpt strange and ghostly shapes as they cover the tower and buildings with ice so thick it takes a hammer to open a door.

One recent storm lasted for twelve days. "Waves pounding the shore actually froze in the air before hitting the ground!" remembers Barney.

It is no wonder lightkeepers who have worked at Green Island want to get away to somewhere less stormy and remote. Families have come and gone over the decades, packing up and leaving after only a year or two, but Keeper Barney loves his island home. He has stayed the course since he arrived a few years ago.

17

A Ton of Gold

During the Gold Rush of 1898, thousands of fortune hunters seeking gold sailed past Green Island on their way to the Klondike region of the Yukon and Alaska, but there was no guiding light on the island. In 1902, a steamer on its way to Alaska ran aground here during a raging storm. Seven men drowned. An engineer inspected the site of the wreck and made a fast decision to build a lighthouse to prevent any more shipwrecks.

Alone, but Never Lonely

The first lighthouse lamp on Green Island was fuelled by whale oil, but today, **solar** panels charge the station's powerful batteries. Built to withstand hurricane-force winds, they are located in a sheltered place on the west side of the island where high winds won't toss them about. **Wind turbines** will soon be installed on the island, and the station, which is currently oil heated, will soon switch to forced-air electric heating, lessening Barney's carbon footprint.

Green Island is on the way to Alaska. *iStock*

Despite dealing with stormy weather and the remote location, Keeper Barney and his assistant enjoy their work.

"We are a special breed of people," says Barney. "Most

My House is a Lighthouse

lightkeepers are somewhat antisocial in general. We like our quiet lifestyle."

And even if friends are just voices on the radio, Barney has made many good friendships from his remote post. "My fondest memories so far are [of] the fellow lightkeepers I have met," says Barney. "We share advice, become close friends, even if we only know each other by a voice on the communications system."

Keeper Barney in front of the Green Island Fresnel lens. *Barney*

Dog Tales

Barney keeps a daily journal of "ramblings," or funny things that happen on the job. His dog, Naulla, a Belgian Malinios, stars in many of these journal entries.

The two have an unbreakable bond, but Naulla often gets up to mischief. "When I'm painting the edges of our walkway for safety, Naulla will walk up, step in the wet paint, and then head off leaving her footprints. Even if I try to shoo her away, she will come back and do it again."

Passing ships and wildlife keep her busy. "She likes to bark and growl at ships, whales, seals, and birds. I have caught my dog a few times taking a cookie down to the water's edge and dropping it into the water for the seals to come get it so she can bark at them. Those seals, in turn, just bark back at her."

19

The Fresnel Lens

Pronounced "fray-nel," these gigantic lenses were invented in 1822 by a French physicist named Augustin-Jean Fresnel specifically for lighthouses. Since this was a time before electricity, Fresnel was trying to find a way to make the candlelight in a lighthouse tower reach farther across the water. His lens featured ridged glass, making each section its own prism. This allowed light to be focused into parallel beams that could be seen from very far away.

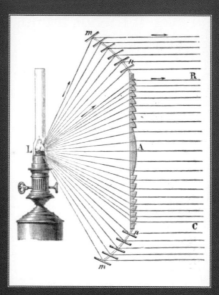

Even after candles and kerosene lamps were replaced with electric light bulbs, lighthouses still used Fresnel lenses because this design requires less glass or plastic to make. Some museums display these treasured Fresnel lamps when they're no longer in use.

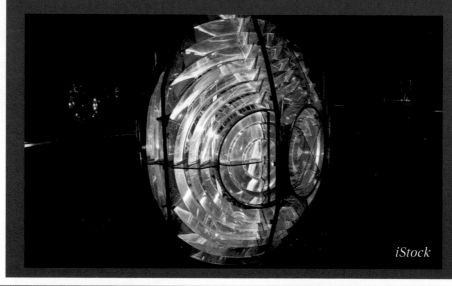

iStock

Things That Go *Thunk* in the Night

With Green Island's history of shipwrecks and its remote and lonely location, Barney admits to being spooked on one occasion.

"When it's eleven o'clock at night and you hear the winds howling through your house, all your lights are off, and you start hearing a *thunk, thunk, thunk* on the walls, you don't know what it is at first…it can keep a person awake for a bit.

"When I first heard the sound, I had no idea what was causing it. I later discovered that a certain species of bird might sometimes fly into the walls [of the lighthouse], disoriented by its light."

The Graveyard Shift

Barney and his assistant divide their day into two shifts. The first one starts at 3:30 A.M. when they send in a local weather report to the Coast Guard, and they repeat the observation and report every three hours until 9:30 at night.

"We share the rest of the work like mowing the lawn, painting, power washing the buildings, and whatever else may come up," says Barney. "We are expected to put in eight hours of work a day.

"The rest of the time is yours to do what you like to keep yourself occupied. But if you have bad weather all week and have been locked up in the house, going out to mow the lawn on a Saturday or Sunday is not a big put out."

The Canadian Coast Guard brings supplies to Green Island. *Lisa Hufnagel*

Lightkeeper Dreams

Can you imagine yourself in this important job? Barney has some advice for you:

"Go for it! Try it for a bit. You may love the job or you may find it's not for you. But if you never try something you will never know—it could be the perfect career for you.

"Had I known of the many opportunities with the Coast Guard when I was leaving school, I may have been here my whole life instead of just after my military career ended a few years ago."

My House is a Lighthouse

Why Staff Light Stations?

Over time, light stations have been automated, and there are fewer keepers to live on site and tend the lights. But Barney knows how important his work is. "If a recreational boater is in trouble near a lighthouse, comes ashore and there is no one to help, then the boater is in a stressful, life-threatening situation," he explains. He knows it falls to him to provide rescue and safe harbour to mariners in trouble.

There are many remote places in Canada that will always have a lighthouse and keeper. Green Island is one of them, beaming forth its promise of safety and security along the coast.

Tiny Green Island is less than two acres in size. *Barney*

CHAPTER 3
Messages in the Stones

Chrome Island, British Columbia

Light characteristic: flashing white every 5 seconds, and a fixed yellow light visible only on the range line.
Foghorn signal: foghorn has been discontinued.

Chrome Island from the air. *Chris Roberts*

"This island is a magical place where mysterious things can happen," says Keeper Leslie about her home on Chrome Island, a tiny isle lying just off Denman Island in the Strait of Georgia.

But Keepers Leslie and her husband, Roger, will never forget their very first lighthouse, a lonely outpost on the Inside Passage of British Columbia.

My House is a Lighthouse

"That lightkeeper's house had no furniture, and it was full of mice," remembers Leslie. "Our welcoming committee told us, 'you guys should get back in the helicopter. There's nothing in the house. You're crazy! Go home.'" But Leslie and Roger were not easily discouraged. "Our kids were grown up. We had been working with the Coast Guard and wanted a change, so we applied for that job, sight unseen," says Leslie. When they arrived, she remembers, "it was snowing white lace paper doilies—the snowflakes were that big! We just started to laugh. We stayed." And twenty years later, they're still in the light-keeping business.

This Island Rocks!

Keepers Leslie and Roger have worked on a few lighthouses since that experience, but Chrome Island truly feels like home. They remember the day they first boated toward the light station to start work, they *did* have a moment of doubt.

"We said to each other, 'Oh, no! What have we done? It's so tiny!'"

Chrome Island is less than two acres in size, but the red roofs of the light station buildings offered a cheerful welcome. And the keeper's house was immaculate.

"No mice," says Leslie. "Everything clean as a whistle!"

Once named Yellow Rock because the sandstone glows golden in the sunlight, the rocks of Chrome Island have stories to tell. Carved into their surface are drawings, called **petroglyphs**,

25

of birds, fish, and humans. The Pentlatch people, an Indigenous group, created this ancient graffiti centuries ago, and here, they kept watch for enemy attacks from the sea.

The first European explorers to this coast carried the smallpox virus. Indigenous people had no resistance to this deadly disease, and thousands died. As a result, the Pentlatch people eventually became extinct, but some Indigenous people today are able to trace their heritage back to Pentlatch ancestors.

Indigenous people carved these drawings centuries ago. *Leslie*

Ghostly Voices

Keepers Leslie and Roger have had their share of mysterious happenings.

"Our island is covered with petroglyphs," says Leslie. "The Pentlatch people kept watch from this island to guard them against warring tribes. There must have been many battles here in the Salish Sea."

My House is a Lighthouse

Leslie recalls how one day, a staff member ran toward her, shouting that she had heard a baby crying.

"It's just the cormorants," Leslie told her, thinking of the wild birds along the cliffs.

Both the principal house (above) and assistant's house (below) look out over the ocean. *Chris Roberts*

"No, no," the woman insisted. "A baby is crying!"

It happened again the next night when they heard the same sound. After some research, they learned that Chrome Island had once been named Dog Island,

and that Indigenous women kept their woolly dogs tied up here. They sheared the dogs' wool to make warm clothing and placed their babies in baskets to keep them safe as they worked.

Could a baby's cry somehow echo into the present from so long ago? Leslie and Roger aren't sure, but they do know that Chrome Island is a mysterious place.

A Cry for Help

This story in the November 19, 2016, edition of the *Times Colonist* newspaper briefly covered a night that could have ended in tragedy if the watchful staff on Chrome Island hadn't come to the rescue.

Leslie and Roger have vivid memories of that evening. "A fellow in the assistant keeper's house was reading quietly, with no music playing and no electronic noise. It was a stormy night. He thought he heard a faint cry for help through the sound of

"This island is magical," says Keeper Leslie. *Leslie*

the wind and waves, and went outside to check. He sighted a young man lying on top of his overturned boat, clutching onto it. The seas were very rough, the waves over six foot high, way too rough for us to launch our boat and get to him.

"We called a mayday and the local ferry launched a fast-response boat, then brought him in to shore here.

"We gave him a hypothermic pad to warm him 'til a life-boat arrived to transfer him to an ambulance. He was lucky we heard him calling out on such a stormy night."

Lucky, indeed!

The successful rescue is yet another reminder of the important work of lightkeepers along this remote coastline.

Ups and Downs

"It's not easy living in isolation," admits Leslie, who believes that lightkeeping is for the "young at heart," but not for the very young.

"It takes a special type of person—isolation is not for everyone. People have a romantic sense that they can come and paint and write a book. But there's always something that needs to be done.

"Even on a nice day something will happen…anything from a sudden storm or an accident, seeing a funnel cloud that will turn into a tornado, or **cumulus** clouds that produce hailstones. Sometimes the supply helicopter is late, or our personal leave might be denied because there is no one to cover for us."

29

Chrome Island Light Station as seen by helicopter. *Alamy Images*

Even with the constant stress and hard work, it is saving lives that gives Leslie and Roger the greatest satisfaction. "It's an unbelievable feeling, that you've saved a life. It makes up for all the bad days when we might be frustrated with life in general and makes us remember the reason we're out here: to keep the mariners safe, all the aviators, kayakers, canoeists, sailboats, and the small crafts."

And for all the hard work, the couple feels lucky to have 360 degrees of ocean

Leslie and Roger's friendly dog, India. *Leslie*

My House is a Lighthouse

view, a beautiful yard and garden, their pet dogs, and the clients they serve.

Community Says "NO!"

A few years ago, Leslie and Roger were warned they would soon be out of a job because the Coast Guard had decided to automate their light station.

"Local people protested fiercely," remembers Leslie, "because they believe that a lighthouse without a keeper might cost hundreds of lives." As a result, Chrome Island will remain staffed. "No guarantees of how long, though," she adds.

The keepers hope people will "see the light" and allow them to carry on their important work of saving lives and helping mariners in distress.

Did you know?

In the nineteenth century, some former keepers were not too happy with their lighthouse home at Chrome Island:

"Beetles, wood mites, wood lice, etc. crawl in the hundreds every day, but chiefly at night, all over the house. They drop into the food cooking on the stove, into our beds, our hair, on to our dining table...both Mrs. Couldery & I are up nearly all night killing these pests to try & keep them down."

From *Guiding Lights: British Columbia's Lighthouses and Their Keepers* by Chris Jaksa and Lynn Tanod (Harbour Publishing, 1998)

CHAPTER 4
Wind Blows in All Directions

Nootka Light Station, British Columbia
Light characteristic: flashing white every 12 seconds.
Foghorn signal: two blasts every 60 seconds.

Each window at Nootka Light Station looks out at Friendly Cove. *Ben Nelms*

"What is this place called?" asked Captain Cook.

The year was 1778, and the explorer had just sailed into the waters now known as Nootka Sound.

My House is a Lighthouse

Hesquiat women canoe into Friendly Cove in 1916. *Library and Archives Canada*

Believing the captain was asking for a place of shelter, the welcoming Mowachaht people called out to him, "Nootka-satl!" meaning they were to sail around to find a safe harbour.

Mistakenly, Captain Cook thought they were calling this place "Nootka" and so that's what the explorer named it. Its true Mowachaht name is *Yuquot*, meaning "where the wind blows in many directions." Some descendants of the Mowachaht Indigenous people still live in the village of Yuquot today.

Time to Slow Down

Keepers Joanne and Mark have kept the Nootka light, a Heritage Lighthouse, for seventeen years and been together for forty-five.

"We're self-starters," says Joanne. "We've been long-haul truckers and lived in the cab, driven forty-eight states and nine provinces. We've skydived. Mark was in the military service.

33

We've done relief work on fifteen light stations in North America."

They stopped wandering for a time to settle down and keep the light at Nootka. The two keepers speak with love and respect for their island home. Their light station looks onto the peaceful waters of Friendly Cove on one side, and the wild waters of the Pacific Ocean on the other.

Mark and Joanne love and respect their island home. *Ben Nelms*

Each day, they watch the eagles and ravens, the whales and the sea otters at play in the waters.

"We dislike crowded places, and love the seclusion and the wild beauty here," explains Joanne. "We're independent."

Never a Free Moment

There is always something that needs fixing to keep the Nootka station going. From time to time the radio will crackle with a distress call from a fisher out at sea.

"We get a lot of boats break down or drifting on the rocks, running out of gas, or boaters that hit the rocks and punch holes

My House is a Lighthouse

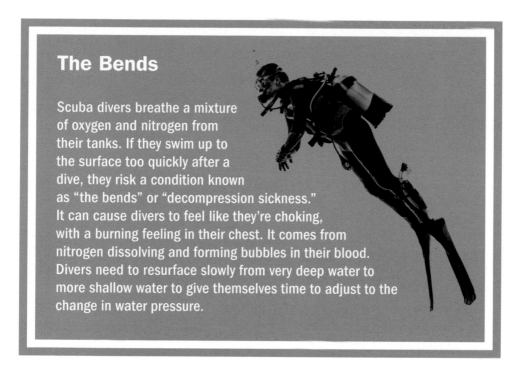

The Bends

Scuba divers breathe a mixture of oxygen and nitrogen from their tanks. If they swim up to the surface too quickly after a dive, they risk a condition known as "the bends" or "decompression sickness." It can cause divers to feel like they're choking, with a burning feeling in their chest. It comes from nitrogen dissolving and forming bubbles in their blood. Divers need to resurface slowly from very deep water to more shallow water to give themselves time to adjust to the change in water pressure.

in the side…or have a heart attack. They arrive soaked or with fish hooks stuck on their body. We get blown-up boats, beached boats, [and] divers with the bends," says Joanne.

The keepers also have to keep watch for bears snacking on blackberries, and cougars lurking in the shadows.

"Mark likes woodworking. I do a lot of crafts—knitting, leatherwork, or sewing. I like to garden and keep the landscape tidy," says Joanne.

The books in the lighthouse library reflect her love of lighthouses. "I like the Dan Connor detective books. There's one called *Black Tide Rising* about a keeper's wife who goes missing, and it's set right here in the cove. The author has described everything perfectly."

The lighthouse today. *Joanne*

Nootka lighthouse in 1934.
Library and Archives Canada

The two make a fine team, keeping watchful eyes around the clock.

"Mark is a nighthawk so he gets the late shift. I'm a morning person, so it all works out," says Joanne. "The first shift is one o'clock in the morning 'til three o'clock in the afternoon. I do the morning weather report for the boats, the visibility, wind, **sea state**, with three hours in between, every three hours, around the clock."

Broken Boats, Broken Bones

The couple has helped many people in distress, not only on the sea, but on land as well. The 44-kilometre Nootka Trail ends here, and hikers have limped into the station with sprains or broken bones. Joanne and Mark bandage limbs and are trained to give First Aid to adventurers on land as well as those on the sea.

"Each window on our station looks out onto a view of Friendly Cove or the Pacific Ocean. We scan

My House is a Lighthouse

for problems," Joanne explains. "One time, a boat close to the horizon broke down. It had no anchor and no way to communicate because its electrical systems went down. They lit a flare, and I happened to be looking out and just caught his flare in time." Joanne is well aware that a boat's electronic devices can fail. Lucky for the mariner that she looked out at that moment "Having a **GPS** on a boat does not make anyone infallible," she says.

Mark climbs to the top of the lighthouse to "keep the lights." *Ben Nelms*

It's not only humans who need rescue. Joanne has fond memories of a stranded bear she and Mark saved during a harsh winter. For six weeks, they

Joanne sits in the radio room to transmit her weather report. *Ben Nelms*

fed the bear and gave her water until the ice melted and she was able to forage once again.

A peaceful summer day at Nootka Light Station. *Ben Nelms*

Down with De-staffing!

Many people believe lightkeepers are no longer needed today because mariners have GPS, satellite phones, and radios. Joanne and Mark know from experience that such tools can fail, and smaller crafts often do not have these tools. So when news came that the Canadian government planned to de-staff all remaining staffed light stations in Canada, Joanne and Mark were determined to stop the automation.

Along with others from the Nootka community, Joanne spoke to a senate committee at a town hall meeting.

"The west coast has twelve thousand miles of coastline that is sparsely populated," Joanne explained. "If there are no keepers to help guide mariners in when they're in trouble, they would perish."

My House is a Lighthouse

Their protests, among those of others, worked to stop the de-staffing. The government backed down. Now, this remote coast continues to have lightkeepers to help those in distress.

Joanne and Mark agree that lightkeeping is not for the young. "Young people would lose their social life, their Wi-Fi. It is a better job for semi-retired people. But the Coast Guard training is good, and marine biology is a rewarding field," says Joanne.

Mark and Joanne are soon planning to move on again, retiring from lightkeeper work. But they will miss their island home.

"It's been like living in *National Geographic*. It's so loud with wildlife," says Mark. "One day I look out and there are four humpbacks right in front of my kitchen. I've seen orcas training their young to hunt seals. When we have the herring spawn in Friendly Cove…everything comes to dine. All the trees are decorated with eagles."

But it's time to pack their boxes. Soon they will welcome the new lightkeepers and say goodbye to Nootka.

Orcas often frolic in the waters off Nootka. *iStock*

For now, life goes on as usual. Joanne sits at her desk in the radio room ready to deliver the first weather report of the day: "Good morning. We are overcast… one-five…west…zero-six… one-foot chop, low southwest." (Translation: the skies are overcast, with visibility for fifteen nautical miles, winds are blowing from the west at six knots, with one-foot waves and low southwest swells.)

It's just another day at Nootka Light Station.

Nootka offers sweeping views of mountains and ocean. *Chris Roberts*

Did you know?

· A nearby church displays stained-glass windows gifted to Canada by the Spanish government in 1957.

· Luna the friendly orca became a viral sensation when he turned up in Nootka Sound after being separated from his pod in 2000.

· *Nuu-chah-nulth* (meaning "all along the mountains and sea") describes about fifteen Nootka bands whose traditional home is western Vancouver Island.

My House is a Lighthouse

CHAPTER 5
Keep Me to Starboard

Boston Light, Boston, Massachusetts
Light characteristic: flashing white every 10 seconds.
Foghorn signal: once every 30 seconds.

Boston Light is the oldest lighthouse in the United States. *iStock*

A boatload of visitors sails toward Little Brewster Island, headed for the famous Boston Light. In the distance, they spy a woman waving a white handkerchief, wearing a long, old-fashioned gown, and a bonnet. It's not a ghost from the past; it's the keeper of the Boston Light.

Keeper Sally polishes the Fresnel lens every month. *US Department of Defense*

If lighthouses could talk, the Boston Light would have fascinating tales to tell. Set afire by gunpowder and fuel oil, fired upon, and witness to hundreds of shipwrecks, this island lighthouse has watched history unfold for over three hundred years. It has much to boast about, and not only because it was the very first lighthouse built in America, in 1716.

There is something else that makes it very special. The Boston Light is the only station in the entire United States that still has a lightkeeper. Her name is Sally Snowman.

Dream Job

"I was born in Boston, and grew up with a view of the Boston Light," says Sally. "Since I was very small, I always imagined keeping that light."

My House is a Lighthouse

She remembers the first time she visited the Boston Light as a little girl. "I first came to visit the island with my dad. We stepped off the dingy onto the beach and looked up to this 89-foot tower and I said to myself, 'When I grow up, I want to get married out here.'"

And when Sally climbed the steps with her dad to the top of the tower, she had the strange feeling that she had done it all before.

"It spoke to me, when I was a child," she says. "I felt at home there. I just knew, somehow, I would be back."

Years later, Sally became a university professor, met her future husband, and realized one of her dreams: the two were married at the Boston Light.

"I started volunteering for the Coast Guard in my spare time," she says. "One day, I saw an ad looking for a civilian to work at the Boston Light." She applied for the position right away. Sally's love for the Boston Light and her interest in history played a big part in what happened next: she got the job!

"I was so surprised I got it," she says. "I couldn't believe it!"

Sally was home at last.

Sally takes pride in being the first woman keeper of the Boston Light.

"I'm the seventieth keeper here. The sixty-nine other keepers that have lived here over the years have all been men. The lighthouse is now 'wo-manned,'" she laughs.

A Lightkeeper's Life

Helping people is Sally's number-one goal. "I want to help show people their way forward, and be of service to them," she says.

Although she is never expected to rescue boaters—that's a job that the Coast Guard now handles—Sally makes sure to always keep a watchful eye on the waters around her. Under her watch, no problem goes unnoticed, as the following tale will tell.

"One day, two dads anchored their boat offshore, and their two kids got in and went for a row by themselves around the island. The winds and waves were a problem, and the kids couldn't get back. I saw them struggling. I got in the lighthouse boat and went out to tow them back [to shore]. They crawled out of their boat, exhausted. The dads had no idea of the danger their kids were in."

While Sally keeps watch for people in trouble on the sea, it's not always humans that she helps—animals sometimes need a helping hand, too.

"A baby seal was sitting up on the rocks but the tide was going out. The mother called from the sea to tell her baby to get off the rocks. Her voice sounded like a dog barking, 'danger!' When I heard that sound, I hurried over to find the baby was crying its heart out. It would have been left high and dry for hours until the tide came back in. I poured buckets of water over the seaweed so it was able to slide down the rocks to the water's edge. The mother came over and said something to her baby, then the two swam away."

My House is a Lighthouse

Spooks at Boston Light

During its three-hundred-year history, lightkeepers of the Boston Light have witnessed hundreds of shipwrecks and the station is believed to be haunted.

"People see spirits all the time out here—the lighthouse is built on an island," says Sally. "Years ago, ships did not have navigation tools. They steered by the stars. On foggy nights, when they turned into the inner harbour at high tide, they sometimes missed the channel and hit the sharp rocky ledges. Ships just cracked open and were lost.

"Boston Light was their guide. 'Keep me to your right, keep me to starboard side, and you'll clear these ledges' was its message. But hundreds and hundreds have died out here."

Is the Boston Light haunted? Many people think so. *iStock*

In 1947, a keeper's wife heard footsteps close behind her as she walked along the shore, but when she turned to see who was following, she saw no one. Later she heard "horrible maniacal laughter" coming from the boathouse. On another night she heard a little girl's sobbing voice calling, "Shaaaadwell!" Other keepers have seen a figure in old-fashioned clothing standing at the tower window.

Any Time to Relax?

A scientist and environmentalist, Sally writes in her spare time. "I wrote a children's book about my lighthouse dog, called *Sammy the Lighthouse Dog.*"

She also keeps busy greeting the hundreds of visitors during the summer months. "We have tours sixteen weeks out of the year, but my job is bigger than greeting visitors," she says. "I can't get bored. Something always comes up from left field. I may have a work plan but it often gets tossed out the window and I wonder, where did the week go?!

"Seagulls are taking over the island, Canada geese are making a mess of the walkways. We pick up the poop and dispose of it. We have a sewage treatment plant that needs inspections. There is always a list of things to do."

The huge Fresnel lens can be a challenge. "I shut the light off once a month to thoroughly clean the lens, and remove fingerprints left by our visitors." Sally usually receives a call from the mainland at this time. "The light is off!" a worried

My House is a Lighthouse

Sally gives a copy of her children's book to Admiral Paul Zukunft, commandant of the US Coast Guard. *US Department of Defense*

landlubber will tell her, reminding her of the importance of the Boston Light to so many people on shore.

Lighthouse Library

Sally is especially interested in stories of women lightkeepers. "I have some fine books about women who [have] kept lights by Candace and Mary Louise Clifford. The three lighthouse keepers that stand out in my mind are: Kate Walker, in New York Harbor; Ida Lewis, in Rhode Island; and Abbie Burgess, a teenage lightkeeper on Matinicus Rock [off the coast of]

Maine. But if I were to choose one book, it would be *Women Who Kept the Lights.*"

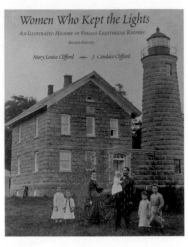

Sally's favourite book. *Cypress Communications*

Guardian Light

To Sally, the Boston Light stands for strength, hope, and peace. "The tower has all the qualities that describe what I want to be," she says. "It's made of rubble stone over two feet thick at the top. To me, that strength stands for integrity. The Boston Light has been lighting the way forward for three hundred years. It's a promise of peace and hope."

Try it!
Would you like a job like Sally's? "If anyone is considering a marine career, I say go for it," says Sally. "Choose a marine career. It will build character, and give skills that are transferable into other careers like the sciences. Bad things are happening in the world, especially around climate change. A marine career builds awareness that we have to focus on the good things, and light the way forward."

The steady light that projects from the Boston Light's tower is powerful and comforting.

"There are twelve separate rays that go out, and if there is any moisture in the air, it really magnifies those beams," explains Sally. "They seem to drop

My House is a Lighthouse

down onto the horizon. It feels so safe. Like nothing is going to harm me. Those are the guardian lights, like beams of hope through the difficult journey of life."

And throughout any difficulty, Sally will continue to maintain and protect her guardian light, shining its way forward into the future.

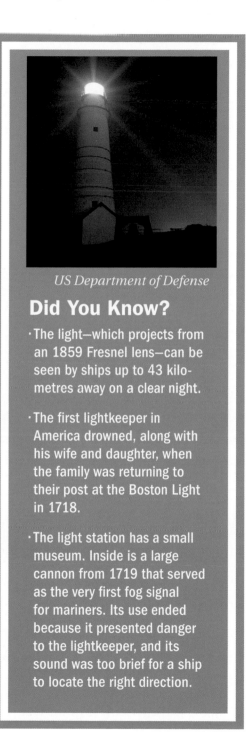

US Department of Defense

Did You Know?

· The light—which projects from an 1859 Fresnel lens—can be seen by ships up to 43 kilometres away on a clear night.

· The first lightkeeper in America drowned, along with his wife and daughter, when the family was returning to their post at the Boston Light in 1718.

· The light station has a small museum. Inside is a large cannon from 1719 that served as the very first fog signal for mariners. Its use ended because it presented danger to the lightkeeper, and its sound was too brief for a ship to locate the right direction.

CHAPTER 6
Feathered Friends

Machias Seal Island, New Brunswick

Light characteristic: flashing white every 3 seconds.
Foghorn signal: foghorn has been discontinued.

Machias Seal Island is a welcome crescent of land for migrating birds. *marinas.com*

"We're not a life-saving station," says Keeper Ralph of the Machias Seal Island lighthouse. But thousands of migrating birds might disagree! The Machias light is a welcome sight, not only for big ships sailing into the Bay of Fundy, but also for tiny songbirds desperate for shelter as they **migrate** south. This treeless 14-acre slab of rock known as Machias Seal Island might not seem like much to anyone else, but to these distressed songbirds, it is a haven of rest and recovery.

My House is a Lighthouse

"Danger Unsafe Landing Area" reads the sign at the entrance to Machias Seal Island. Visitors have to be very careful on the rocks. *Chris Sears*

Songbirds migrating thousands of kilometres to their winter homes face a dangerous journey. The stress of constant flying and lack of food along the way challenges their physical abilities. When you add severe weather and strong winds to the already-dangerous trip, it's not uncommon for the little birds to become so exhausted they simply "fall out" of the skies mid-journey to rest and gather strength.

Mind If We Drop By?

"We're sitting on the Atlantic flyway, so we get a full range of migrating birds, night-flying, and day-flying," says Ralph, who has kept the Machias Seal Island light for years.

Hundreds of songbirds rest during their long journey south. *Ralph Eldridge*

"We're like a convenience store; many birds drop out of the voyage to rest and feed. Some stay for a few hours, a few hang around for several days. Many gather around the lighthouse and lightkeeper's house at night. During the night flights, my house would fill with birds if I left the windows open," he laughs.

Ralph respects the birds' need for space and rest, but he keeps his windows closed. Seeing thousands of birds gathered in one place may be a wildlife photographer's dream, but Ralph cautions people not to approach the birds during **fallout**.

"The birds are utterly exhausted and everyone should resist the temptation to get close or otherwise disturb them. I keep my distance," he says. "I am careful to avoid further stressing these birds. Many are near to death. When I take pictures, I sacrifice [photo] quality to avoid harming them. They desperately need to sleep, rest, and feed, not to waste energy avoiding people. That urge to get 'just one close-up' could well cost the bird its life."

My House is a Lighthouse

Puffin Paradise

Apart from the occasional tourist boats that visit in the summer, Machias Seal Island might be called a lonely place. It is a barren, rocky island with no trees. Sometimes the fog is so thick, you might think you are hanging in the clouds. But if you lived here, you wouldn't be lonely. There are an estimated seven thousand pairs of puffins for company—the largest nesting colony of puffins on the Atlantic coast south of the **Gulf of St. Lawrence**.

This puffin enjoys a tasty snack of shrimp. *Dr. Tony Diamond, UNB*

Who's at the Door?

One dark night during a thick fog, a former keeper heard a tap at his front door. He looked out but saw no one there. Moments later, it came again: *tap, tap, tap*. Once again, the keeper opened the door. No one.

He was just about to close the door when he looked down. There stood a baby puffin. It had marched to his house, confused by the light, as it was working its way down to the sea.

Safe Spot for Birds

Machias Seal Island is officially known as a bird sanctuary. The Canadian Wildlife Federation manages it, and the numbers of species sighted here could fill a book: Arctic tern, common tern, black tern, roseate tern, eiders, shearwaters, puffins, razor-bill auks, kittiwakes, storm petrels, spotted sandpipers, guillemots, savannah sparrows, cormorants, gannets, gyrfalcons, peregrine falcons, kestrels, merlins, murres, herring gulls, laughing gulls, great black-backed gulls, loons...the list goes on!

A Peaceful Dispute

The island lies smack dab between Canada and the United States, close to Grand Manan Island in New Brunswick and also the coast of the state of Maine.

The island's proximity to Maine has caused a peaceful disagreement between the two friendly countries. During the First World War, American Marines were stationed on the island at Canada's invitation, keeping watch for German U-boats (submarines) entering the Bay of Fundy. Today, ownership of the island is in dispute. The Canadian Coast Guard keeps a presence at this Heritage Lighthouse by protecting the bird-breeding grounds and supporting Canada's claim to the island.

My House is a Lighthouse

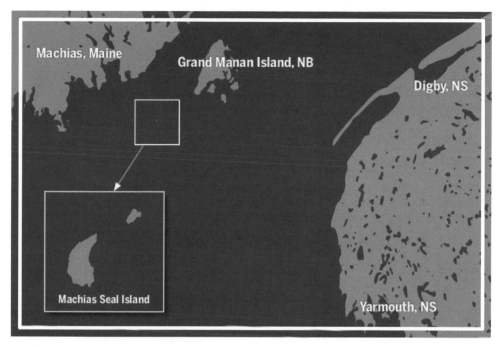

Machias Seal Island lies smack between the borders of Canada and the United States. *iStock*

What Does it Take to Keep the Lights?

"You must be self-sufficient to keep the lights," Ralph says. "Be able to work unsupervised, and know what you have to do and how you do it. There's repetition in the work. The independence is something I like about it."

Having a marine background gives Ralph an understanding of the weather and the environment, but the work demands organizational skills as well.

"You have to get a handle on ordering yearly supplies, check various systems, maintenance and repair work," he says. "I can deal with whatever equipment routines that the station has."

What's in Your Lighthouse Library?

"A good dictionary," Ralph laughs. "Everyone has their own likes and dislikes, but for my personal selection—a fair number of reference books."

You can be sure that bird books are among those in Ralph's collection, too.

This gull has lots to tell Keeper Ralph.
Ralph Eldridge

A beautiful sunset illuminates the lighthouse. *Bob Ballard*

"Books that deal with the natural world," he adds. "With a place like this, you get the opportunity to see the breeding colony of puffins up close and the life cycle of their chicks. Most people never get to see this."

The Perfect Friendship

If you are lucky enough to pay a visit to this tiny island, you will be welcomed by the barking of seals. As you walk along, you will see hundreds of birds around you, squawking and flapping. Acrobatic terns wheel and dive above, while puffins burrow into rocky crevices, and razorbills push their way into the gaps between rocks.

From wooden blinds, you will be up close and personal with all kinds of bird species hopping about and sunning themselves. Be respectful. Birds need friends, and Machias Seal Island, with its keepers and warden, will always offer protection, safety, and shelter—the perfect friendship.

In order not to startle the resting birds, visitors can view them from these photography "blinds." *Michael Weaver*

CHAPTER 7
Sorry! No Puffins Here

Puffin Island, Newfoundland and Labrador
Light characteristic: flashing white every 5 seconds.
Foghorn signal: 3-second blast, silent for 27 seconds.

On a clear day, visitors can view Puffin Island from Greenspond. *Craig*

"Sure gets spooky here at night," says Keeper Craig about his lonely outpost on Puffin Island, on the northern shores of Bonavista Bay, Newfoundland and Labrador. "When the foghorn blows on a foggy night, you can't see anything, only hear the wind and the ocean."

My House is a Lighthouse

Craig is used to life on remote shores. He grew up in the small community of Badger's Quay near Bonavista Bay. Badger's Quay is only a few kilometres from Puffin Island, and the monthly helicopter brings Craig back and forth in no time at all. He has kept the Puffin Island light station for twenty-five years.

"Work wasn't plenty in Badger's Quay," says Craig of his decision to leave the town. "My dad was on the Canadian Coast Guard, he encouraged me, and I took a Marine Emergency Training course to qualify me for work on the ships. Then this light station came open, and my mother said, 'Son Craig could do that.' And here I am!"

In spite of its name, there aren't actually any puffins on this tiny, treeless spit of land. "We see wagtails, little small birds, grassy birds, but no big birds, just smaller birds, beachy birds," explains Craig.

The whole island is just over a kilometre in length, and is only accessible by helicopter or boat. The small islands here are as plentiful as their curious names: Batterton, Ship, Newell's, Wing's, Pig, Maiden, Groat.

The larger island close by, Greenspond, is the

The lighthouse on Puffin Island in 1900.
The Rooms Provincial Archives

Sorry! No Puffins Here

oldest inhabited **outport** in Newfoundland. The very first light-house on Puffin Island was built in 1873!

A Day in the Life

Craig and his assistant keeper share two shifts; each one pulls a twelve-hour shift to ensure the lighthouse is staffed 24/7. "One does days and one does nights [so] we don't see each other except for a few shifts," Craig explains.

The day's routine involves checking the solar panels and the electrical equipment.

Foghorn

When the weather is foggy, some-times boats and ships can't see the light of a lighthouse. In these conditions, a foghorn blares a loud sound to warn sailors that rocky shores are nearby. The very first foghorns were bells that the lightkeepers clanged in foggy weather, or sometimes even small cannons! Eventually, a Scottish man living in New Brunswick named Robert Foulis invented a steam-powered foghorn in the

Library and Archives Canada

1840s. He heard his daughter practicing piano one foggy night but could only hear the lower notes. He thought a device that made a deep, low sound would carry farther over the water. Early versions of his foghorn had to be cranked by hand, but these days they are fully automatic.

My House is a Lighthouse

At the end of his twenty-eight-day shift, Keeper Craig and his dog Molly board the helicopter back to the mainland. *Adam Randell*

"If there's a fog on the go, we make sure the foghorn's goin'. We don't send reports to Environment Canada, but we look after the fishermen. We get a forecast and relay it on to them. And there's always cookin' and cleanin' to do."

A helicopter drops off food supplies each month. Craig and his assistant plan the menus with care and make sure there are enough groceries to last until the next helicopter delivery. If they run short, there are always wild ducks to hunt. "Get a bird, get it in the roaster to make a meal [like] a duck or a turr," says Craig.

For hobbies, Craig likes to build Coast Guard ship replicas, model lighthouses, and even a dartboard case. "There's not too much I haven't tried, to tell you the truth," he says.

Sorry! No Puffins Here

All This for a Tasty Treat

This wind-tossed rock has seen a few shipwrecks, but the keepers are not equipped to get involved with rescue work. The seas here are too rough for keepers to risk their own lives. Like all keepers, Craig is in contact with the **skippers** of fishing boats who need wind and tide information as they navigate around these small islands. Skippers rely on the keeper for **ice reports** so they can avoid the danger of being stuck among the floes.

But there was one incident where Craig and his assistant were able to help, and not a moment too soon.

Every year starting in November, turr-hunting season brings hunters to the waters near Puffin Island. On cold winter mornings, the keepers can hear the near-constant *boom* of 12-gauge shotguns.

At sea in their open boats, turr hunters endure stinging salt spray and biting cold. For them, it's worth it just for the pleasure of some roasted turr at the end of the day.

Early one November morning, Craig and the assistant keeper caught the motion of something out in the bay, swinging back and forth.

"We was around the light station doing some work," says Craig. "We look across the bay and seen a boat out there, a paddle stuck up in the air, waving back and forth with something black or green, a rubber coat on top. They were out after birds. Turr hunters. We run out and sees they were in a big jam."

Newfoundland turr make a tasty meal for hunters. *iStock*

The boaters were soaked to the skin, and their boat was close to capsizing in the rough waves. Craig and his assistant keeper motored out to them and towed them back into shore and safety. Hopefully the grateful hunters enjoyed a good roasted turr dinner after that freezing adventure on the sea!

No Room For Three

There came a moment when the keeper of Puffin Island almost needed rescuing himself. It all began when a polar bear became curious about the Puffin Island light station.

That morning, Keeper Craig felt a pair of eyes looking at him as he stood at the kitchen window. Outside, he saw a large shape lumbering around the station.

"A polar bear swam down from the Northwest Territories and came ashore on Puffin. We saw him outside the window coming across near the solar panels," he related.

63

Craig and his assistant went outside to watch it, but when the bear came too close, they ran into the house to keep an eye on it from the windows. It roamed around the house for a while, but after a good sniff didn't turn up any food, the bear soon had enough of lighthouses and their elusive keepers. It left to swim toward Greenspond. To this day, Craig always keeps a watchful eye out for polar bears. You never know when that bear might pay a return visit!

Igor Pays a Visit

Craig has seen some rough weather, but nothing like Hurricane Igor, which struck Newfoundland in 2010. When the bad weather began, Craig became worried about his family in Badger's Quay. He works twelve-hour shifts in a rotating schedule of twenty-eight days on and twenty-eight days off. He was just in the middle of his on-shift at the light station. Could his family manage without his help? Would the wicked wind knock out their power and bring down trees on the house? He wished he could be with them.

"I've seen some real storms," says Craig, "but the one I remember the most was Igor—I come through the roughest time I ever seen. The pathway between the house and the buildings was covered with rocks thrown down [from the sea], the same size as footballs."

Indeed, with winds gusting to 172 kilometers per hour and waves up to 25 metres high, the storm washed out roads and bridges on Bonavista, and destroyed hundreds of homes.

My House is a Lighthouse

Hurricane Igor (2010) caused much damage to roads in Bonavista, as well as to the light station. *Chad Fisher*

Happily, Craig's family managed to stay safe through the storm, but these situations remind him that he often has to miss out on important events at home.

"What I like least about this job is being away for six months of every year, and not only to take care of emergencies at home. I miss important gatherings. That's the only bad part about my job."

In his early years at the station, he had only a telephone/fax machine, but today, with internet and cellphone service, Craig can keep in touch with his family. Craig almost lost his job in 2009 when the Coast Guard began to de-staff lighthouses across Canada. But by 2010, with public protests and a Senate review, it was decided that the work of lightkeepers is vital to marine safety. Craig was happy to stay on.

"I love my job, but it can't get much better than hearing that chopper coming to pick me up, having the feeling of coming home," Craig says. "It gives you a lump in your throat to hear the chopper at the end of twenty-eight days."

Sure, Give It A Try...

Craig knows lightkeeping is not for everyone. But he encourages anyone who is interested in ships or the sea to join the Coast Guard.

"Go ahead and do it because they treat me the best, I loves it...still loves it. Not everyone can live on an island—leave and come out—but if you work on the Coast Guard ships, you have twenty or thirty people along with you. So sure, I recommend it to everyone. It's nothing but the utmost, the best stuff!"

If you ever visit Greenspond Island, go to the very furthest reach, and look over the water. If the day is not foggy and the sea is calm, you can see the Puffin Island light and know that Keeper Craig is there keeping watch over the slate-grey seas of Bonavista Bay.

Did you know?

· Puffin Island Lighthouse is one of the twenty-three staffed light stations in Newfoundland and Labrador. Newfoundland has the most staffed lighthouses anywhere in Atlantic Canada.

· The Atlantic puffin is the official bird of Newfoundland and Labrador.

CHAPTER 8

Beacon at the Edge of the World

Cape Race, Newfoundland and Labrador

Light characteristic: flashing white every 7.5 seconds.

Foghorn signal: two blasts every 51 seconds.

Cape Race sits at "the edge of the world." *Tourism Newfoundland*

"Lightkeeper is the right job for me!" says Keeper Michael of Cape Race, Newfoundland. "You're always watching over the ocean for people's safety, listening to the VHF [very high-frequency radio]. You have a good purpose in life."

Keeper Michael has kept the light at Cape Race for eighteen years and is proud of its history. Designated a Heritage Lighthouse and a National Historic Site, the station has a fascinating claim to fame.

Cape Race and the *Titanic*

The first transatlantic wireless transmission was received at St. John's Signal Hill in December 1901 by Guglielmo Marconi, and three years later a **Marconi wireless** station was built at Cape Race. In 1912 it played an important role in helping to rescue passengers from the sinking RMS *Titanic*.

RMS *Titanic* sets sail from Southampton, England, in 1912. *Public domain*

In April of that year, a radio message came to Cape Race from the *Titanic*—an urgent distress call from a doomed ship: "CQD CQD CQD SOS Titanic Position 41.44 N 50.24 W. Require immediate assistance. Come at once. We are struck by a berg. Sinking."

My House is a Lighthouse

Radio operator Walter Gray helped to coordinate rescue efforts with the nearby passenger ship RMS *Carpathia* and other ships in the area. The whole world listened for radio updates from Cape Race. The *Titanic* story became the world's first "breaking news" of the twentieth century. Today, the wreckage of the *Titanic* still lies on the ocean floor some 350 nautical miles from Cape Race.

A Dreadful Place

Stormy, fog-bound, and with a front-row seat to drifting icebergs, Cape Race sits at the edge of the world. It was the last sight of land for military troops crossing the Atlantic during the two World Wars. It was the first sight of land for refugees sailing to Canada dreaming of a new life.

Keeper Michael knows the importance of having a human presence at the light station. Flat and treeless, Cape Race is

The Cape Race light station is often shrouded in thick fog. *Asst. Keeper Cliff*

blanketed in fog for an average of 158 days a year. When the wind is southerly, waves slam against the tall shale cliffs and drench the barrens above with sea spray. Called "a dreadful place" by navigators, this rocky outcrop has cost thousands of lives and shipwrecks throughout history.

"We have rough weather," says Michael. "Every winter we have a big storm, no shelter from the wind. We get it all. The

Waves slam the tall shale cliffs at Cape Race. *Asst. Keeper Cliff*

seas are very rough, waves nine metres high." Despite the messy weather and lonely existence, Michael loves his job.

Rescue in the Night

Rough weather tested the grit of Captain Hailey, the very first lightkeeper at Cape Race. In 1856, just settled in his newly built lighthouse, the captain faced a severe test. Fog had drifted in, so thick the station light could not shine through it. Without

My House is a Lighthouse

a visible light to warn sailors of the rocky shore, a tragedy occurred. The *Welsford*, a ship travelling from New Brunswick to England, smashed into the reefs and rocks at the bottom of the Cape Race cliffs.

After that accident, Captain Hailey pleaded for a stronger light and a louder foghorn. Ninety-four more ships were lost over the next fifty years. Over two thousand lives were lost.

Cape Race provides warm light on a cold winter's night. *Asst. Keeper Cliff*

At last, a powerful foghorn was installed along with the largest Fresnel lens ever built. Its beam of light was strong enough to cut through thick fog and mariners could see it from a long distance away.

Cape Race finally boasted one of the most powerful lights of its day.

Beacon at the Edge of the World

A Day in the Life

Though the weather is changeable, Keeper Michael's daily routines remain the same. "I get up same as everyone else, have breakfast, and we monitor the light from the house every two hours, and keep the log," he says. "Me and the assistant [Keeper Cliff] take turns cooking. Visitors coming and going all the time."

"What I like most about my job is knowing I have a purpose," he says. "I don't dislike one thing. Not one thing. No one wants anything to happen. You just do the best you can."

Visitors to Cape Race enjoy exploring the six buildings that mix together old and new. The old lightkeeper's home and fog alarm building date from 1900, while the new lightkeeper's dwelling was built in 2000.

"We're on a National Historic Site," says Michael, "so we meet different people, comical, friendly, that helps pass the time, I enjoy their stories, people comin' and goin'."

A Bit of Advice

While Michael's main work is to warn ships away from the rocks, he welcomes the many visitors at this historic site. He says that to do a good job, a lightkeeper must have good people skills.

"My advice is, be able to interact with other people. Your manner has a lot to do with your success. It helps to be able to talk to people, get along. We meet strangers and tourists, we share the work. My fondest memories are of interactions with other people I've met, making friends with the people I've worked with."

Ready and Watching

While automation has replaced many lightkeepers around the world, Michael is certain Cape Race will always have a keeper to watch for those in distress on the sea.

"One time, just recently, a sailboat was just drifting along, lost, and we put a call in to the other boats to come save 'em, and they did—just in the nick of time! Sure, there's technology to warn ships now, but you can't replace the human being. No, there's no replacement for that."

A busy lightkeeper family in 1954 at Cape Race. *Library and Archives Canada*

In a Nutshell

Keeper Michael is dedicated to fulfilling his important work on Cape Race. "It's like you have a purpose, you know what your job is for the day. That's what I most like about this work.

Visitors can see all kinds of wildlife at Cape Race. Keeper Cliff tries to photograph as many as possible, like this caribou, red fox, and snowy owl. *Asst. Keeper Cliff*

My House is a Lighthouse

Knowing I have a good purpose in life."

If you walk on the Titanic Trail to Cape Race, you will find barrens that have never grown a tree, and can watch caribou and wild birds. From the cliffs you might spy whales feeding on capelin and herring in the waves below. And you will hear the curlew, a bird whose haunting song conveys the spirit of Cape Race—this wild and remote place at the edge of the world.

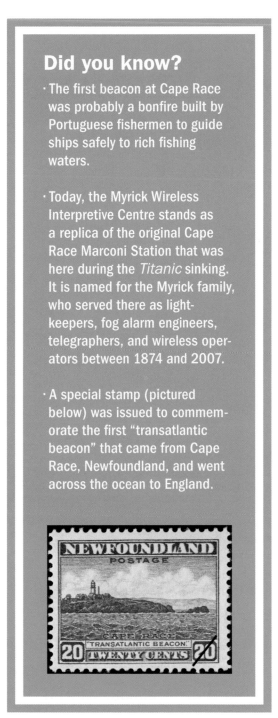

Did you know?

· The first beacon at Cape Race was probably a bonfire built by Portuguese fishermen to guide ships safely to rich fishing waters.

· Today, the Myrick Wireless Interpretive Centre stands as a replica of the original Cape Race Marconi Station that was here during the *Titanic* sinking. It is named for the Myrick family, who served there as light-keepers, fog alarm engineers, telegraphers, and wireless operators between 1874 and 2007.

· A special stamp (pictured below) was issued to commemorate the first "transatlantic beacon" that came from Cape Race, Newfoundland, and went across the ocean to England.

Beacon at the Edge of the World

CHAPTER 9
A Blizzard of Gannets

Cape St. Mary's, Newfoundland and Labrador

Light characteristic: flashing white every 5 seconds.
Foghorn signal: three blasts every 27 seconds.

The Cape St. Mary's light sits atop towering cliffs that also serve as a wildlife reserve. *Sheila Antle*

"Lots of people say to me, 'I wouldn't be out there by myself,' but I don't mind," says Mary, keeper of the St. Mary's Lighthouse. After all, she has thousands of feathered friends for company.

The area is known for its nesting birds that migrate here in the thousands during the summertime. It is home to the

Cape St. Mary's Ecological Reserve, where northern gannets nest side-by-side with guillemots, murres, and kittiwakes. It makes for a very loud and very messy patch of rock.

This Heritage Lighthouse sits at the top of towering cliffs that are blanketed in fog for two hundred days of the year.

Fog as Thick as Pea Soup

Keeper Mary took over the lightkeeper job when her husband, Mike, retired after thirty-five years on the lights. With so much fog, both Mary and Mike's priority has been to make sure the foghorn is working at all times.

"Our foghorn has five fog detectors. It's a semi-automatic station. The horn comes on when it detects fog, but if it's not working, we can turn it on manually," explains Mary.

The lighthouse at Cape St. Mary's before a fresh coat of white paint. *Frank King*

Her husband, Mike, remembers one particularly bad storm when a thick fog lasted for twenty-nine days straight.

"We got used to hearing the foghorn for all that time. After the storm, we counted thirty-six rocks hurled through the lighthouse windows by winds, breaking nine panes of glass." They hadn't even heard the breaking glass over the constant drone of the horn!

Where Are the Fish?

Cape St. Mary's lighthouse was built on the Avalon Peninsula in 1858 to guide fishers on their journey to the once-rich fishing grounds around Cape St. Mary's. There's an old saying used by fishers: "Cape St. Mary's pays for all." It meant that if ever fishers had a bad day, they could make up their losses at the Cape, where the fish were always plentiful.

So famous were the fishing grounds that there is a well-known song, written by Otto P. Kelland in 1947, describing the fishers' yearning to be back at Cape St. Mary's.

> *Take me back to my western boat*
> *Let me fish off Cape St. Mary's*
> *Where the hog-down sail*
> *And the foghorns wail*
> *With my friends the Browns and the Clearys*
> *Let me fish off Cape St. Mary's*

My House is a Lighthouse

In 1992, the Canadian government shut down all cod fishing off the coast of Newfoundland. Overfishing was causing the cod population to collapse. The **moratorium** continues today, and commercial cod fishers no longer cast their nets here. But in the past, thousands would make the trip to the waters of Cape St. Mary's, once one of the richest fishing grounds in the world.

A Lighthouse In the Dark

The Cape St. Mary's Lighthouse was built in 1859, but no warning **beacon** flashed in its tower until a year later. Although the lamp started its voyage to Cape St. Mary's from Scotland in August 1859, storms and gales were so fierce that the lamp was

The powerful light at Cape St. Mary's beams out across the ocean. *Dreamstime*

A Blizzard of Gannets

placed in storage until the following summer. At last, calmer winds and seas allowed a safe delivery.

Leave It To Us!

It is unusual for a woman to keep the lights at Cape St. Mary's. Traditionally, it has been considered "a job for a man." But today there are three women keepers who share the duties year-round.

"There have been no women working here in the past," says Mary. "But this opening for lightkeeper came up, and three women applied. We took a test and interviewed, and were placed according to the order we came. I was given the September to December shift—the other two work January to April, and May to August. We all have four-month shifts."

Keeper Mary enjoys her four-month shifts. She kept up the family tradition of keeping the lights after her husband retired. *Sheila Antle*

My House is a Lighthouse

The "Bird Stack" is home to thousands of birds. *Sheila Antle*

Clifftop Walks

Mary enjoys walking the trail that stretches across sub-Arctic tundra to Bird Rock. Here, a sea stack of sandstone over twenty-two metres tall gives viewers a close-up look at the nesting birds.

Separated from the cliff by a deep chasm that plunges to the sea below, the "Bird Stack" is a seasonal home to thousands of birds that swoop and dive above, build their nests side by side, and tend to their eggs. Visitors can watch the seabirds' flying maneuvers, which ends up looking like a blizzard of whiteness.

The northern gannet population increases to twenty-four thousand during the summer breeding time. Kittiwakes and

81

Visitors enjoy watching the flying maneuvres of the northern gannets. *iStock*

murres add their wild calls, the resulting cacophony rising to a pitch that almost wipes out the sounds of the wind and waves.

"No matter what the weather is like, you can still see and hear them," says Mary.

Just the Usual

Mary performs the regular work of a lightkeeper. "We work eight-hour days, make sure the horn is working, and the light. We do a coastline search walk along the cliff. There's always something to keep us busy."

"I like the work," says Mary. "It's so interesting, it's good to be keeping people safe on the ocean, lots of people still depend on the horn and the lights. I do a weather report, write in the logbook. The foghorn cuts in [at] different times during the day.

"We get lots of visitors from May to September. Only a few come during my shift, but there are lots of rabbits and foxes visiting. July is a good month to see the whales passing by."

Mary agrees the work of a lightkeeper is not for everyone. "If you have the personality for it, and don't mind being alone for some stretches, it's a fine job."

And if there are no people, feathered friends can be good company!

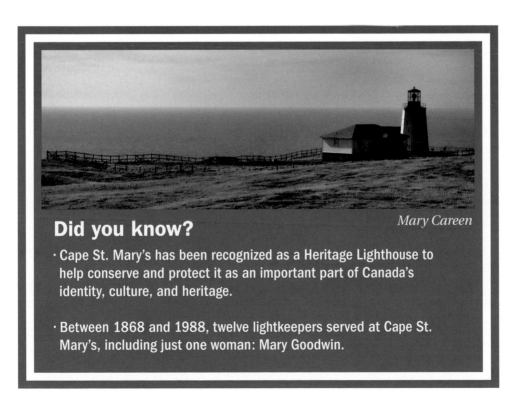

Mary Careen

Did you know?

· Cape St. Mary's has been recognized as a Heritage Lighthouse to help conserve and protect it as an important part of Canada's identity, culture, and heritage.

· Between 1868 and 1988, twelve lightkeepers served at Cape St. Mary's, including just one woman: Mary Goodwin.

A BLIZZARD OF GANNETS

CHAPTER 10
The Lights of Fortune Bay

Fortune Head and Green Island, Newfoundland and Labrador

Fortune Head light characteristic: flashing white every 5 seconds.
Foghorn signal: every 27 seconds.

Green Island light characteristic: flashing white every 10 seconds.
Foghorn signal: every 56 seconds.

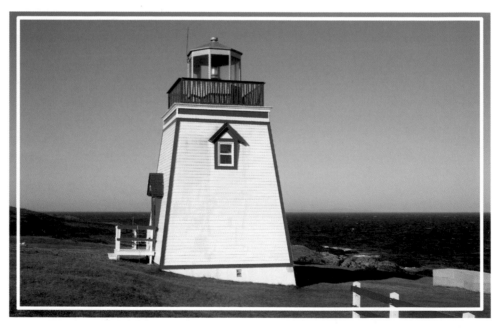

Fortune Head Lighthouse offers a cheerful welcome. *Kraig Anderson*

Sleeping with the Light On

Not many children can say they are able to sleep with a light flashing every ten seconds through their bedroom window, but Keeper Calvin can. When he was little, he lived at a lighthouse station. Calvin spent some of his growing-up years with his family on Green Island in Fortune Bay where his father, William, kept the light. It lies in the stretch of ocean called Fortune Bay, between the Burin Peninsula in Newfoundland and the French islands of Saint Pierre and Miquelon.

When Calvin turned five, he left the island to live with his family on the mainland, in the town of Fortune. There, he started school. But he never forgot his first island home.

"I have lots of good memories about growing up at Green Island," says Calvin. "My brothers and sisters climbed the rocks, swam, built a log cabin in the woods. We caught capelin, picked blueberries, marsh berries, partridgeberries, and raspberries close by. In the winter, there were lots of places to slide."

Just like Dad

During his young life on the island, Calvin had seen many mariners in trouble. He felt proud to help his dad whenever he was able. Now all grown up, Calvin lives in the town of Fortune and has a family of his own.

It is no surprise that when the keeper at Fortune Head Light Station retired Calvin took over. Today he is lucky to live at

The Lights of Fortune Bay

The road leading in to the town of Fortune. *Lee Shelp*

home with his family and it takes just a short drive every day to reach the light station, where he keeps watch and tends to the lights.

An International Friendship

Fortune Head Lighthouse overlooks Fortune Bay, a body of water once fished by fishermen from Portugal, who came for the plentiful cod. They called it *Fortuna,* meaning "harbour of good fortune," but luck has sometimes failed mariners on these waters.

At the far entrance of Fortune Bay is a group of eight islands known as Saint Pierre and Miquelon. Belonging to France, they sit on an international boundary line and represent a long friendship between France and Canada.

The waters around Saint Pierre and Miquelon can be dangerous in rough weather. Once referred to as the "Mouth of

My House is a Lighthouse

Hell," more than six hundred ships have been caught on rocks and sunk there since the seventeenth century.

On the Atlantic Canada side, lightkeepers on nearby Green Island watch for mariners from Saint Pierre and Miquelon who might find themselves in the middle of the sudden storms that sweep the area.

One such storm was so severe a bulk carrier ship, the MV *Flare*, broke in two separate pieces, and twenty-one crew members died in the waters near the islands.

Saint Pierre and Miquelon are located off the coast of Newfoundland, but are actually part of France. *iStock*

All the Time in the World

Fortune Head light station was a lonely spot until fossils were discovered in its rocks and cliffs. Since that time, Keeper Calvin meets visitors from around the world who come to search the reserve and stop by the lighthouse for a chat. At the Fortune Head Geology Centre, visitors can see exhibits of fossils found exposed in the rocks and dating back millions of years—541 million, to be exact!

In winter, the tourists are gone, but Calvin is used to Newfoundland's wild coastal weather, where seas pound the rocky cliffs and blizzards create whiteout conditions.

"Some storms, we get waves fifty feet high," says Calvin. "We can't see through the windows for seas slapping against them. Winters are bad—lots of wind and snow. Last year, I got stuck for a few hours at the station because of the snow."

From his perch at Fortune Head light station, Calvin can see the passenger ferry pass by on its way from the town of Fortune to the islands of Saint Pierre and Miquelon. The ferry captain relies on the weather reports from the lightkeepers before making the journey across the bay.

Save Our Souls

Calvin keeps a sharp watch for fishers and small boats in trouble. If he sees anyone in distress he radios the Coast Guard for

Fortune Bay has eight islands all together. *Kraig Anderson*

My House is a Lighthouse

help. He will never forget the time he helped save four people when he worked on nearby Green Island (Fortune).

"We rescued a family from Saint Pierre a good many years ago. Had a call one time in the morning around eight o'clock. Three kids and a man and woman were on their way to Langlade from Saint Pierre, and the boat overturned. We could hardly see them in black fog.

"We walked around Green Island and there came a break in the fog, just for a moment. We saw the boat upside down, floating around the ocean. We went out in our flat-bottom boat, and picked them all up."

Sadly, one little girl died.

Visitors enjoy the view from the helipad at Fortune Head. *Tourism Newfoundland*

"She was only seven years old," says Calvin with great sadness. Accidents like these are sometimes part of day-to-day life when you live and work at a light station.

Say No!

In 2009, the government announced it would gradually de-staff all lighthouses across Canada, including those at Fortune Head and nearby Green Island. Upon hearing this news, communities around Fortune Bay rallied together and began peaceful protests. These protests were loud enough to change the government's plans and the keepers were allowed to stay and continue their important work.

It is this strong community support that is so important to keepers like Calvin. He is certain there will always be lightkeepers watching over the waters of Fortune Bay, helping boaters to get home.

Did you know?

· The treacherous waters of Fortune Bay have seen more than 600 shipwrecks since 1800. Some people still call it "Gallows Bay."

· For fourteen years, there was no road to connect the light station with the town of Fortune. Lighthouse children lived in the town while their lightkeeper fathers lived at the lighthouse. At last, a four-kilometre dirt road was built in 1968.

My House is a Lighthouse

CHAPTER 11
Touched by the Sunrise

Cape Spear, Newfoundland and Labrador
Light characteristic: three white flashes every 15 seconds.
Foghorn signal: every 60 seconds.

The Cantwell family has kept the lights at Cape Spear for over a century. Here, Keeper Gerry (now retired) watches the sun set. *Brian Carey*

When Gerry was a boy, he announced to his parents: "I'm not going to be a lightkeeper." He had just been watching his favourite television show about a police officer. "Maybe I'll be a cop, instead."

Gerry's family was surprised to hear this, for there have been Cantwells at Cape Spear for over a century. Family tradition eventually won Gerry over and he changed his mind. "It holds an affection with you," says Gerry of his lighthouse home. "If you live here, you're close to the sea. It's a beautiful spot. If you have the chance to go, you'll see why so many visit Cape Spear."

The Cape Spear light station stands in St. John's Harbour at the most easterly point in North America; the very first place on the continent to be touched by the sunrise each day. Built in 1836, this historic station eventually became one of the many across Canada to be automated and de-staffed. In 1997, Keeper Gerry became the last keeper and the last of the Cantwells to work on the station. He kept the light for thirty years and watched it transform from a lighthouse with no running water or electricity to a fully automated station.

Gerry still speaks of his old home with fondness. "Cape Spear is home, and that's the way it is; when you're born into something, it's part of your life," he says.

Thanks, Your Highness!

Gerry's ancestor, James Cantwell, became the very first of a long line of Cantwells to keep the light at Cape Spear. He won the post by performing a good deed for a royal prince.

In 1836, a ship carrying Prince Henry of the Netherlands lost its way in the harbour's thick fog. Along the narrow channel into port lie seven huge rocks affectionately named

My House is a Lighthouse

Chain, Merlin, Ruby, Seal, Prosser's, Cahill, and Pancake. It's a tricky route to navigate even in the best of weather.

Nineteen-year-old harbour pilot James Cantwell rowed out with other boats to search for the lost ship. He was first to spy it through a gap in the fog,

Children play on the windy grounds of the original Cape Spear light station in 1936. *Library and Archives Canada*

and with great care piloted it safely into port.

"Name your reward," said the grateful prince.

"Your Highness, I want to be lightkeeper at Cape Spear," replied James.

In 1846, when the light's first keeper retired, James got his wish. And so began the Cantwell family tradition of keeping the Cape Spear lights.

Old and New

Built in 1836, the first lighthouse at Cape Spear had to be chained to the rocks after a strong gale lifted it right off its foundation. Over the years, generations of Cantwells have witnessed changes to their lighthouse home. **Kerosene** replaced the old seal oil lamps, then a Fresnel lamp welcomed mariners to port. Its triple flash could easily penetrate thick fog.

93

Touched by the Sunrise

A new **diaphone** fog alarm replaced the **fog trumpet**. The lighthouse station included a light tower that rose from the roof of the keeper's home. Later, a separate concrete, six-sided lighthouse tower was built alongside the house. Both still stand.

The fog trumpet at Cape Spear, similar to the one pictured here from Nova Scotia, was replaced by a diaphone foghorn. *Library and Archives Canada*

Gerry was part of a large family unit at Cape Spear. "My mom was a new-comer there. She taught school at the Cape and loved it, met my dad, Frank Cantwell, and stayed," he explains. "I had five brothers and sisters. We all lived there [and] went to school [there] 'til it was time for high school. We made sure to keep the friends we made. There were only two families living at Cape Spear, and if you didn't get on with your playmates you'd have nobody to play with."

A Family Affair

As a boy, Gerry followed his dad around, learning how to run a lighthouse.

"I was five, maybe even four years old when I went with my dad down in the fog alarm building," says Gerry. "It was quite loud.

My hearing is suffering from that today. Then when I got old and strong enough to start these engines, my father expected me to do it and I did it. It's a family affair. You did what you had to do around your home."

If You Can't Fix It, Live with It

Most light stations in Newfoundland cannot be reached during bad weather. Being located out on the rocks in the North Atlantic Ocean with no roads to connect with other towns, means travel by helicopter or boat is the only way in or out… and only in good weather.

"The land twists, and all the dangerous rocks around Newfoundland shores and along the Strait of Belle Isle make rescues difficult. Cape Spear is on a point of land sticking out into the North Atlantic, you can't launch a boat for a rescue attempt. But in good conditions, some stations are still able to retrieve persons in trouble."

"I was raised to expect anything," says Gerry. "You've got to be prepared. There could be a storm, a fire, even sickness and death. You had to live with it till the time you could get someone there. These were harsh locations along the Newfoundland coast. But you knew what you were getting when you went there."

Just Flick a Switch

Cape Spear was automated in 1997. It became a National Historic Site and a Heritage Lighthouse, and Gerry retired from lightkeeping after thirty years of living or working on

Sunrise at Cape Spear. *Tourism Newfoundland*

the station. He is the last Cantwell and the last keeper to keep the lights at Cape Spear.

"Lightkeeping has changed since my ancestors first worked the lights at Cape Spear," says Gerry. "Everything is automatic, now. The horn starts and stops by itself. The light is left on all day, or works on a switch. There's very little to do other than maintaining the equipment, the small things. Today it's all about tourists."

The original lighthouse building and the lightkeeper's residence have been restored to the period of 1839, and are open to the public. Although Gerry is officially retired now, he still volunteers at Cape Spear, showing tourists around his old home and thrilling them with stories of his boyhood and his time as lightkeeper.

My House is a Lighthouse

CHAPTER 12
Not Just a Flash in the Dark

~~~~~~

Lighthouses are treasured places but sadly, many de-staffed lighthouses and dwellings across North America become damaged, vandalized, or destroyed because there are no protections in place.

The Heritage Lighthouse Protection Act was passed in 2008 to protect lighthouses and recognize their importance to Canada's nautical history. A similar act was passed in the year 2000 in the United States. Community groups work to preserve the heritage of abandoned or automated lighthouses across North America and keep these treasures safe from harm. As a result, such lighthouses have become repurposed as inns, museums, or tourist centres.

People who work to protect them know that lighthouses are more than just flashes in the night. Each lighthouse has a story to tell, an experience to share of life on the rough edges, of souls lost, or lives saved from the hungry seas by a brave lightkeeper.

So if, on some dark night, you see a light flashing at the end of a point of land, or on a high clifftop or rocky shore, think about the lightkeeper and the family who once lived there.

Imagine the many mariners who found shelter, comfort, and safety on its shore.

And listen.

Among the calls of gulls and curlews, you can almost hear the happy sounds of the lightkeeper's children playing on the rocks, or the ghostly cry of a mariner seeking safety from the storm.

My House is a Lighthouse

Acknowledgments

A host of people aided and empowered me during the raw stages of this book. My gratitude goes out to all the lightkeepers and former keepers, gift shop managers, librarians, historians, photographers, researchers, scientists, archivists, and Coast Guard personnel. The lightkeepers themselves took time to speak to me during their busy days, and cared enough to ask as many questions about me as I asked about them. If I've forgotten anyone it's only because of my messy notes and not because their contributions are any less important.

Thanks to: Kirby Adams; Kraig Anderson, Lighthouse Friends; Tasha Andrews, Fisheries and Oceans Canada; Sheila Antle; Robert Appel; Rory Banks; Murielle Boudreau, Tourism New Brunswick; John Boutilier, Newfoundland Region Coast Guard; Helena Burke; Craig Burry; Damien Busi, Parks Canada; The Canadian Register of Historic Places; Gerry Cantwell; Mary Careen; Brian Carey; Julia Cook; Paul Cranford; Tim Cyr, Nootka Island Lodge; William H. Day; Janet Denstedt, Old Salt Box Co.; Elinor DeWire; Dr. Tony Diamond, UNB; Cliff Doran; Dan Duffett; Terry Duffett; Holly Dunham; Bonny Durnford; Ralph Eldridge; Justine Etzkorn, Library and Archives Canada; Christopher Fitzgerald, Canada Light Station Operations St. John's; Josh Green, NB Provincial Archives; Pattifeather Greenham, Cape Mudge; Tim Harrison, Lighthouse Digest; Barney Hynes; Keeper Karen; Lisa Kerr, Pacific Region Coast

Guard, Heather L. Kirby, Fisheries and Oceans Canada; Catherine Lawton; Valerie Matheson; Rebecca Meunier, Parks Canada; Chris Mills; Laurie Murison; Larry Peach; Laurie Perrin, L'Arche Museum, Saint Pierre and Miquelon; Sally Snowman; Jennifer Ready; John Summers, Cape Spear; Calvin Thornhill; Joanne and Mark Tigglman; Sharon Topping; Melanie Tucker, Newfoundland Provincial Archives; Kelly-Ann Turkington, Royal BC Museum; Sam Whiffen, Canadian Coast Guard; Michael Ward; Linda White, Archivist, Memorial University; Leslie Williamson; John Willis, *CoastGuardNews*; Carolyn Woodward; Karen Zacharuk.

A big thank you also goes out to Whitney Moran, managing editor at Nimbus, who recognized this book's merits and took it on. Thanks also to editor Emily MacKinnon and publicist Kate Watson.

Further Reading

Picture Books and Fiction

A Picnic at the Lighthouse by Rebecca North

Anne's House of Dreams by L. M. Montgomery

Gracie, the Lighthouse Cat by Ruth Brown

Hello Lighthouse by Sophie Blackall

Sammy, the Boston Lighthouse Dog by Sally Snowman

Non-fiction

Lighthouses of Atlantic Canada by David Baird

Lighthouses of North America: Beacons From Coast to Coast by Sylke Jackson

Lights of the Inside Passage by Donald Graham

The Lighthouse Keeper's Daughter by Lenorc Skomal

The Lightkeeper's Menagerie: Stories of Animals at Lighthouses by Elinor DeWire

Women Who Kept the Lights by Mary Louise Clifford

Glossary

ALN phone — Automated Light Station Network. A telephone network that connects all lighthouses in a given area.

anemometer — an instrument to measure wind speed.

beacon — a visible warning or guiding point, usually displayed in a tall, easy-to-see location, such as a lighthouse.

Canadian Coast Guard — a fleet of government ships and helicopters used for search and rescue, security, ocean pollution reporting, traffic control, ice breaking, communication of weather and sea conditions, and training.

cumulus clouds — fluffy, white clouds.

daymark — since you can't see a lighthouse's beacon in the sunshine, light towers are painted different colours and patterns so sailors can tell one apart from the other and figure out their position.

diaphone — a horn-like noisemaking device that emits a deep, powerful tone that can carry across a long distance. Used as early foghorns.

fallout — fallout happens when migrating birds have to interrupt their journey because of bad weather and stop to rest somewhere. Usually it's because of strong wind, which forces the birds to burn more energy and causes them to get tired more quickly.

foghorn — modern foghorns are powered with a solar-charged battery. They are activated by sensors that measure the density of water vapour in the air.

fog trumpet or fog whistle — a warning sound to ships that was operated by a small coal-fired engine. The engine compressed air inside a cylinder on top of which was a reed horn or a locomotive whistle. The compressed air was released through a valve and passed through the whistle or reed trumpet to "blow the horn."

Fresnel lens — invented in 1822 in France, the ridged design of the glass lens focused the beam in lighthouse lamps, which allowed them to reach a much greater distance.

funnel cloud — a long, cone-shaped cloud extending from the base of a cloud. If the funnel cloud touches land, it becomes a tornado; if it touches water, it becomes a waterspout.

GPS — Global Positioning System. A satellite-based navigation system, and an important aid for ships and small boats.

Gulf of Saint Lawrence — the area of water between mainland Newfoundland and Quebec, extending down to the Maritimes.

Heritage Lighthouse — a lighthouse receives a heritage designation based on its aesthetic and architectural qualities, its historical importance, and its legends and lore.

ice report — a forecast about the presence and thickness of ice in waters ships are trying to navigate.

Inside Passage — a route for ships and boats that weaves through the many small islands along the coast of British Columbia and Alaska.

kerosene — mostly used as fuel for airplanes these days, kerosene was once popular for lighting lamps, lanterns, and lighthouses.

Marconi wireless — a means of transmitting messages through Morse Code using radio waves instead of wires.

My House is a Lighthouse

mayday — a distress call used in radio communications to report an emergency, repeated three times in a row. The word comes from the French *m'aider*, meaning "help me."

migration — the regular seasonal movement of birds (usually north–south) between breeding grounds and wintering grounds.

moratorium — a temporary ban on an activity.

nautical mile — a unit of measurement over water. It is slightly longer than a land mile because it factors in the circumference of the earth.

petroglyphs — images made in rock by picking or carving, often associated with prehistoric and Indigenous peoples.

reef — a ridge of jagged coral, rock, or sand just below the water surface.

sea state — the condition of the sea, relating to wave height and wind.

skeletal tower — a modern lighthouse with an open frame, maintained by the Coast Guard with no keeper on site. It has a single stationary flashing light powered by solar-charged batteries.

skipper — the captain of a ship or boat.

solar-powered — a panel converts the energy of sunlight into electricity.

wind turbine — a large wheel that is rotated by the wind to generate electricity.

Index